KU-447-107

Russia

Sue Townsend and Caroline Young

Heinemann LIBRARY

501 251 182

501251182

 www.heinemann.co.uk/library
Visit our website to find out more information about **Heinemann Library** books.

To order:
☎ Phone 44 (0) 1865 888066
▤ Send a fax to 44 (0) 1865 314091
▣ Visit the Heinemann Bookshop at www.heinemann.co.uk/library to browse our catalogue and order online.

First published in Great Britain by Heinemann Library, Halley Court, Jordan Hill, Oxford OX2 8EJ, part of Harcourt Education.

Heinemann is a registered trademark of Harcourt Education Ltd.

© Harcourt Education Ltd 2003
First published in paperback in 2004
The moral right of the proprietor has been asserted.

All rights reserved. No part of this publication may be reproduced, stored in a retrieval system, or transmitted in any form or by any means, electronic, mechanical, photocopying, recording, or otherwise, without either the prior written permission of the publishers or a licence permitting restricted copying in the United Kingdom issued by the Copyright Licensing Agency Ltd, 90 Tottenham Court Road, London W1T 4LP (www.cla.co.uk).

Editorial: Nancy Dickmann, Andrew Solway and Jennifer Tubbs
Design: Jo Hinton-Malivoire and Tinstar Design Limited (www.tinstar.co.uk)
Illustrations: Nicholas Beresford-Davies
Picture Research: Catherine Bevan
Production: Séverine Ribierre

Originated by Dot Gradations Ltd
Printed in China
by WKT Company Limited

ISBN 0 431 11728 4 (hardback)
07 06 05 04 03
10 9 8 7 6 5 4 3 2 1

ISBN 0 431 11735 7 (paperback)
08 07 06 05 04
10 9 8 7 6 5 4 3 2 1

British Library Cataloguing in Publication Data
Townsend, Sue & Young, Caroline
Russia. – (A World of Recipes)
641.5'123'0947
A full catalogue record for this book is available from the British Library.

Acknowledgements
The publishers would like to thank the following for permission to reproduce photographs: Corbis: p. 5; Gareth Boden: all other photographs.

Cover photographs reproduced with permission of Gareth Boden.

The publishers would like to thank Raisa Goutsal of The Russian Fairytale Delicatessen and Anna Hart for their assistance with the preparation of this book.

Every effort has been made to contact copyright holders of any material reproduced in this book. Any omissions will be rectified in subsequent printings if notice is given to the publishers.

Contents

Key

* easy

** medium

*** difficult

Words appearing in the text in bold, **like this**, are explained in the glossary.

Russian food

The Russian Federation, as we now call Russia, is the biggest nation in the world. It stretches across two continents (Europe and Asia). It takes a train seven days to travel from Moscow, on one side of the Federation, to Vladivostock, on the other. Russia is divided by the Ural Mountains, which form the boundary between its European and Asian parts.

In the past

The first people to live in Russia were tribes called the Slavs, in the 8th century. They gave the area the name 'Rus'. During the 1200s, Batu Khan, grandson of the ferocious Genghis Khan, led the Tatar armies from the east and conquered Russia. The Tatars ruled for the next 200 years. One of Russia's earliest kings, or Tsars, was Ivan Grozny (Ivan the Terrible), who killed his own son in a burst of anger. Russia remained cut off from the rest of the world until the 1600s, when Peter I (Peter the Great) visited western countries to find out about their ideas. When Russia fought several costly wars during the 1800s, people began to question the royal family's power and wealth. In 1917, the people overthrew the Tsar in a revolution. The Union of Soviet Socialist Republics (USSR) was formed, ruled by **communists**. In 1991, the USSR collapsed and the Russian Federation was born.

▲ *This market in Bryansk, Russia, has a small range of bread for sale.*

Around the country

Russia's climate is very extreme. The far north of Russia is called the tundra. It is an icy, treeless plain, where the ground is almost permanently frozen. South of the tundra is a band of coniferous (evergreen) forest, known as taiga, then **deciduous** forests. Grassy plains, called steppes, stretch for thousands of kilometres across the middle of Russia. Farmers grow different grains, fruit and vegetables, and millions of sheep and cows graze on the land. Around the Caucasus Mountains, the land is especially **fertile**. In the south, in hot, desert areas, it hardly ever rains.

Russian meals

Russia is so huge that people cook very differently from region to region. Most Russians eat a lot of bread with their meals, and might have bread, cold meat or caviar (see page 6) for breakfast. Lunch is usually the main meal of the day, and often includes pickled vegetables. A Russian dinner might begin with lots of different starters, called *zakuski*. Tea, called *chai*, is very popular in Russia. It is kept hot in a metal urn, called a *samovar*.

Ingredients

savoy cabbage

beetroot

buckwheat flour

sorrel

mushrooms

onions

soured cream

potatoes

curd cheese

quark

salmon caviar

caviar

cherries

carrots

dill

Beetroot

The fat, purply-brown root of the beetroot plant is a vegetable. It is usually cooked in its skin and peeled afterwards, to stop its colour running out. You can only buy fresh beetroot at certain times of the year, but it is always available in plastic packets, or pickled in vinegar.

Buckwheat flour

Buckwheat seeds are **roasted** and **ground** to make a dark-coloured flour with a slightly earthy flavour. You can buy buckwheat flour in packets from most large supermarkets or from health-food shops.

Caviar

Caviar is made with the eggs (or roe) of the sturgeon fish. Fish eggs are very small and have a soft jelly-like 'shell'. There are different types of caviar, including greyish beluga caviar from the beluga sturgeon. This costs hundreds of pounds for a small jar. Supermarkets sell pink salmon caviar, which is cheaper. Use lump-fish roe if you cannot find caviar. Look for both in a chilled food cabinet or at a fishmonger's.

Curd cheese

Curd cheese is a soft, creamy cheese. It is often used in dessert recipes, because it does not have a strong cheesy taste. Most supermarkets sell it in tubs, but you can use fat-reduced cream cheese or quark, if you cannot find curd cheese (see below).

Dill

Dill is a feathery green herb with a flavour a little like liquorice. It is **chopped** and added to recipes, or used to **garnish** recipes. Large supermarkets sell fresh dill.

Quark

Quark is a soft cheese made from skimmed milk. It contains very little fat. It has a soft, smooth texture and a slightly lemony flavour. Look for it in the chiller cabinet of large supermarkets.

Sorrel

Sorrel is a dark green leafy plant that looks very like spinach. It has a tangy, slightly lemony flavour. Sorrel is often added to salads and soups. Look for it in large supermarkets, but use spinach if you cannot buy sorrel.

Soured cream

Soured cream has had special **bacteria** added to it to make it turn sour. Do not use old cream that has gone off. Soured cream tastes slightly sharp, but still creamy. If you cannot find soured cream, use single cream and stir in 1–2 teaspoons of lemon juice instead.

Before you start

Kitchen rules

There are a few basic rules you should always follow when you are cooking:

- Ask an adult if you can use the kitchen.
- Some cooking processes, especially those involving hot water or oil, can be dangerous. When you see this sign, take extra care or ask an adult to help.
- Wash your hands before you start.
- Wear an apron to protect your clothes.
- Be very careful when you use sharp knives.
- Never leave pan handles sticking out, in case you knock them.
- Use oven gloves to lift things in and out of the oven.
- Wash fruits and vegetables before you use them.
- Always wash chopping boards very well after use, especially after chopping raw meat, fish or poultry.
- Use a separate chopping board for onions and garlic, if possible.

How long will it take?

Some of the recipes in this book are quick and easy, and some are more difficult and take longer. The strip across the right-hand side of each recipe page tells you how long it takes to prepare a dish from start to finish. It also shows how difficult it is to make – each recipe is * (easy), ** (medium) or *** (difficult).

Quantities and measurements

You can see how many people each recipe will serve at the top of each right-hand page. You can multiply or divide the quantities if you want to cook for more or fewer people.

Ingredients for recipes can be measured in two different ways. Metric measurements use grams and millilitres. Imperial measurements use ounces and fluid ounces. This book uses metric measurements. If you want to convert these into imperial measurements, see the chart on page 44.

In the recipes you will see the following abbreviations:

tbsp = tablespoon   g = grams   cm = centimetres
tsp = teaspoon   ml = millilitres

Utensils

To cook the recipes in this book, you will need these utensils (as well as essentials, such as spoons, plates and bowls):

- plastic or glass chopping board (easier to keep clean than a wooden one)
- food processor or blender
- large frying pan
- 18 cm heavy-based non-stick frying pan
- measuring jug
- flameproof casserole dish with lid
- sieve
- small and large saucepans with lids
- set of scales
- slotted spoon
- baking sheets
- baking parchment
- colander
- sharp knife
- grater
- 9 cm and 6 cm round pastry cutters
- square muslin cloth or clean tea towel.

 Whenever you use kitchen knives, be very careful.

Borsch (Beetroot soup)

Russian cooks have made *Borsch* (pronounced *boar-sh*) for centuries. There are many different versions, but each one contains beetroot. For Borsch, the beetroot is **peeled** so that its red juice colours the soup. You can use raw or **boiled** beetroot, but not beetroot pickled in vinegar.

What you need

1 beef or vegetable stock cube
2 beetroots (raw, if available)
1 onion
2 medium potatoes
200 g green or white cabbage
1 tbsp butter
2 tsp wine vinegar
 or lemon juice
4 tbsp soured cream

What you do

1 Crumble the stock cube into 1.2 litres hot water and stir well.

2 Peel the beetroots and **grate** them over a bowl.

3 Put the beetroots into a large pan and add the stock water. **Simmer** for 10 minutes.

4 While the beetroots are cooking, peel and finely **chop** the onion.

5 Peel the potatoes. Cut them into 1 cm wide slices, then into 1 cm wide strips and then into 1 cm cubes.

6 Cut off the cabbage stalk and throw it away. **Shred** the cabbage.

(!) 7 Heat the butter in a pan over a medium heat. **Fry** the onions for 4 minutes, until they are softened. Add the potatoes and cook for 3 minutes, stirring from time to time.

8 Add the onion, potatoes and cabbage to the beetroot mixture. Bring to the boil, **cover** and simmer for 15 minutes.

9 Add some salt and pepper, and the wine vinegar or lemon juice.

10 Spoon the soup into four bowls and add a tablespoon of soured cream to each. Serve hot or cold, with white bread if you want to be really Russian!

11

Blini (Buckwheat pancakes)

Blini are small, round pancakes made with buckwheat flour. In Russia, people traditionally serve them as a starter, with soured cream and either caviar (see page 6) or smoked salmon. Most caviar is very expensive, so try serving *blini* with lump-fish roe, which most large supermarkets or fishmongers sell.

What you need

75 g buckwheat flour
pinch of salt
1 sachet easy-blend yeast
1 tsp sugar
180 ml milk
1 egg
2 tbsp vegetable oil

Serve with:
100 g smoked salmon
   or 4 tbsp caviar, salmon
   caviar or lump-fish roe
8 tbsp soured cream

What you do

1 Sift the buckwheat flour and salt into a bowl. Add the yeast and sugar.

(!) 2 Heat the milk very gently in a saucepan, until it feels the same temperature as your finger when you dip it in.

3 Beat the egg lightly in a bowl. Pour the milk and egg into the flour mixture, stirring until there are no lumps.

4 Cover the bowl with clingfilm and leave in a warm place to rise for 2 hours.

5 Turn the oven on to its lowest setting and put a baking tray in to warm.

ⓘ6 Heat the oil in a non-stick frying pan. Add 2 tbsp *blini* mixture to the pan so that it forms a small, round pancake.

ⓘ7 **Fry** for 2–3 minutes over a medium heat on each side.

8 Put the cooked *blini* onto the warm baking tray, cover with foil and keep warm in the oven while you cook the rest of the mixture. The mixture should make 20–24 pancakes.

9 Arrange a few *blini* on each person's plate with some smoked salmon, soured cream or caviar, if you like. Serve straight away.

Potato and sorrel soup

Winters in Russia can be extremely cold, so thick, hot soups are a good way to warm up. Cooks use potatoes, onion and carrots as the main ingredients for this recipe. Use spinach if you cannot buy sorrel.

What you need

1 onion
2 large potatoes
1 vegetable stock cube
225 g sorrel or spinach
1 tbsp butter
4 tsp soured cream

What you do

1 **Peel** and finely **chop** the onion.

2 Peel the potatoes. Cut them into 2 cm wide slices, then 2 cm wide strips and then into 2 cm cubes.

3 Crumble the stock cube into 600 ml hot water and stir well.

4 Put the sorrel into a large bowl of cold water. Tip it into a colander over the sink to **drain**. Pull off any tough stalks.

5 Heat the butter in a large saucepan over a medium heat. Add the chopped onion and **fry** for 3–4 minutes, until softened.

6 Add the potatoes and stock. **Cover** and **simmer** for 15 minutes. Cool for 10 minutes, leaving the liquid in the pan.

7 Tip the sorrel into another pan, cover and cook gently for 2–3 minutes, until the leaves are droopy. You do not need to add any more water.

8 Using a slotted spoon, put the sorrel into a blender or food processor. Add 5 tbsp cooking liquid from the potatoes and **blend** until smooth.

9 Now add the rest of the cooking liquid and potatoes, and blend until smooth.

(!) 10 Pour the soup back into the saucepan. Add salt and pepper to taste, heat thoroughly and spoon into serving bowls.

11 Add 1 tsp of soured cream to each bowl. Serve with crusty bread.

Devilled eggs

Russian people serve a selection of small savoury snacks, called *zakuski* (pronounced *za-KOOS-key*) before a special meal – or, sometimes, instead of a main meal. They are usually beautifully presented and **garnished**. This recipe is one of the most popular *zakuski,* and makes an ideal starter.

What you need

4 eggs
4 tsp butter
4 tsp double cream
1 tbsp fresh parsley
3 canned mushrooms
1 tbsp prawns
1 tbsp anchovy fillets

To garnish:
2 prawns
2 sprigs fresh parsley
1 anchovy fillet

What you do

(!) 1 Put the eggs into a pan. Carefully cover them with **boiling** water. Bring the water back to the boil, and then **simmer** for 8 minutes.

(!) 2 Using a slotted spoon, lift the eggs out of the pan, crack the shells and put them into a bowl of cold water to cool for at least 10 minutes.

3 Take the shells off the eggs and cut each egg in half lengthways. Using a teaspoon, carefully scoop out the egg yolks, and put each one into a separate cup.

4 Divide the butter and cream between the four yolks. **Chop** the parsley finely.

5 Cut two **slices** of mushroom and keep them to use as a garnish. Finely chop the rest of the mushrooms, then the prawns and then the anchovies.

6 Add the mushrooms to one egg yolk, the prawns to another, the anchovy to the third and the chopped parsley to the fourth.

7 Chop each egg yolk with a knife against the side of the cup to mix everything together.

8 Using a teaspoon, spoon one of the four fillings into each of the eight egg-white halves.

9 Garnish each egg with a prawn, a slice of mushroom, a sprig of parsley or a little anchovy, depending on which filling it contains.

10 **Chill** for 30 minutes before serving with Liver pâté (see page 18) and Vegetable pastries (see page 24) for a typical selection of *zakuski*.

17

Liver pâté

Pâté is a smooth meat paste, usually made from liver. In Russia, people eat this pâté with bread as a starter, or *zakuski* (pronounced *za-KOOS-key*). They sometimes eat it with sliced, cold meat and pickled vegetables, such as beetroot or gherkins. It has a fairly strong flavour, so you may not need too much of it on your bread.

What you need

450 g pigs' or
   calves' liver
200 g streaky
   bacon
1 carrot
1 onion
½ tsp nutmeg

What you do

1 Rinse the liver under cold, running water. On a chopping board, cut out any white bits of flesh or fat.

2 Cut the liver into 3 cm sized pieces.

3 Cut any rind off the bacon and throw it away. Cut the bacon into small pieces.

4 **Peel** and finely **chop** the carrot and onion.

5 Heat a frying pan over a medium heat. **Fry** the bacon, carrot and onion for 3 minutes, stirring from time to time.

6 Using a slotted spoon, lift out the bacon. Add the liver and cook for a further 5 minutes. Let it cool down.

7 When cool, spoon the liver mixture and the bacon into a blender or food processor, and **blend** until smooth. Add the nutmeg, and salt and pepper to taste.

8 Spoon the mixture into a small bowl. Flatten the surface with a knife. **Cover** with clingfilm and **chill** for 3 hours.

9 Serve with rye bread, crusty bread or fingers of toast, and salad.

Georgian-style chicken casserole

Chicken is an important ingredient in many Russian main dishes. It is usually **roasted** or cooked slowly with vegetables in a casserole. This recipe is from the republic of Georgia, formerly of the Soviet Union, between Russia and Turkey.

What you need

4 chicken quarters
  (either leg or wing)
2 onions
25 g butter
3 tbsp fresh coriander
1 chicken stock cube
2 tbsp tomato purée
1 tbsp white
  wine vinegar

To garnish:
sprig of fresh
  coriander

What you do

1 **Preheat** the oven to gas mark 5/190 °C/375 °F.

2 Pull the chicken skin down off the chicken pieces. Cut it off around the leg or wing tip with some scissors.

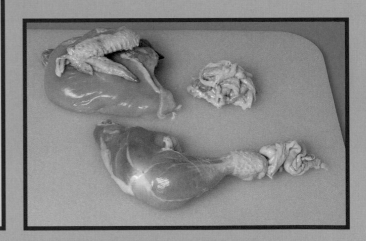

3 **Peel** and **slice** the onions.

(!) 4 Heat the butter in a flameproof casserole dish over a medium heat until it has melted. Add the chicken pieces and cook for 3 minutes on each side, until they are browned.

(!) **5** Lift the chicken out of the dish on to a plate. **Fry** the onions in the casserole dish for 3 minutes.

6 **Chop** the coriander.

(!) **7** Crumble the stock cube into the dish, stir in 400 ml hot water, tomato purée, coriander, vinegar, and salt and pepper to taste. Bring to the **boil**.

8 Lift the chicken back into the dish. Put the lid on tightly and cook in the oven for 2 hours. Stir every 30 minutes, and add extra hot water if it is drying up.

9 Before serving, garnish with coriander. Serve with potatoes or rice and vegetables.

Stuffed pumpkin

Pumpkins and squash keep well for several months, if they are stored in a cool, dry place. People keep them for cooking during the long, cold Russian winter, when few things grow. This recipe makes a warming main dish.

What you need

75 g long-grain rice
1 medium pumpkin
    (approx 1.7 kg)
    or 4 small pumpkins
    or squash
3 tbsp fresh coriander
75 g raisins
3 tbsp butter

What you do

(!) 1 Put the rice into a saucepan. Pour in 1.2 litres **boiling** water. Bring it back to the boil and stir well. **Cover** and **simmer** for 20 minutes.

(!) 2 Using a sharp knife, **slice** the pumpkin's top off. Do not throw it away.

3 Scoop out the seeds with a spoon, and throw them away.

4 **Preheat** the oven to gas mark 5/190 °C/375 °F.

5 **Chop** the fresh coriander.

6 **Drain** the rice and put it back into the hot pan. Add the raisins, butter, coriander, and some salt and pepper, and stir well.

7 Spoon the rice mixture into the pumpkin.

8 Put the top on the pumpkin and **bake** for 1 hour, or until the pumpkin flesh is so soft that a knife point goes into it easily.

9 To serve, you can either scoop out the filling with a spoon or cut everyone a slice of stuffed pumpkin.

MORE STUFFED VEGETABLES

Russian cooks also stuff other vegetables, such as turnips, peppers and tomatoes.

Piroshki (Veg table pastri s)

Piroshki (pronounced *peer-ash-KEY*) are small envelopes of pastry filled with minced meat, vegetables or curd cheese. They are popular all over Russia, where they are served as a tasty starter.

What you need

For the pastry:
175 g plain flour
   plus 1 tbsp flour
   for **dusting**
pinch of salt
1 egg
60 g butter
2 tbsp soured cream

For the filling:
½ onion
½ carrot
50 g cabbage
50 g curd cheese
   or quark
1 tsp caraway seeds
1 egg

What you do

1 **Sift** the flour and salt into a bowl.

2 **Beat** the egg lightly with a fork. Cut the butter into small pieces.

3 Stir the egg, butter and soured cream into the flour with a fork. Using your hands, pull the mixture into a ball.

4 Sprinkle a little flour over a work surface. Stretch the dough out, fold it over and press it down with your palm. **Knead** in this way for 2–3 minutes, until the dough is smooth. Wrap it in clingfilm and **chill** for 30 minutes.

5 **Peel** and **grate** the onion and carrot.

6 **Shred** the cabbage and put it into a small saucepan.

7 Cover the cabbage with **boiling** water, **cover** the pan and **simmer** for 2 minutes.

8 **Drain** the cabbage well, let it cool and then **chop** it finely.

9 In a bowl, stir the curd cheese, onion, carrot, cabbage, caraway seeds, and some salt and pepper together.

10 **Preheat** the oven to gas mark 7/200 °C/400 °F. Dust a work surface with 1 tbsp flour. Roll out the dough until it is 3 mm thick.

11 Use a 6 cm round pastry cutter to cut out 24 rounds.

12 Put a teaspoonful of the filling into the centre of each round.

13 Beat the second egg and brush it around the edges. Fold over each round and pinch the edges together.

14 Line a baking sheet with baking parchment, and lay the pastries on it. Brush them with a beaten egg.

15 **Bake** for 15 minutes. Allow to cool a little before serving.

Shashlyk lamb kebabs with onions and tomatoes

Traditionally, these kebabs were cooked on an open fire and served to Russian nobles with the ingredients speared on swords. They are called *shashlyk* (pronounced *shash-leek*), which means kebab. This recipe comes from the republic of Georgia. If you can, cook them on the **barbecue**, Russian-style.

What you need

600 g boneless leg
   of lamb
2 onions
75 ml white wine
   vinegar
black pepper
2 tomatoes

To garnish:
2 tomatoes
a few lettuce leaves

What you do

1 Cut the lamb into 3 cm chunks and place in a bowl.

2 **Peel** the onions and cut them into wedges. Add them to the lamb.

3 Stir the vinegar into the bowl and add some black pepper. **Cover** and **chill** the meat in this **marinade** for at least 4 hours.

4 Cut the tomatoes into six wedges. First, thread a piece of lamb, then onion and then tomato on to four metal skewers, until everything is used up.

5 **Preheat** a grill to medium hot. **Grill** the *shashlyk* for 5 minutes, then turn the skewers and cook for a further 5 minutes. (Turn them earlier if they start burning.)

6 Cut into one chunk of lamb to see if it is cooked, not pink. Cook for a little longer if you prefer your lamb well done.

7 Serve with salad as a light lunch, garnished with tomato wedges and lettuce.

Potatoes baked with soured cream

Many savoury Russian recipes include soured cream, which is called *smetana* in Russian (pronounced *smee-et-AR-na*). Here, it is added to potatoes to give this dish a moist, creamy flavour. Serve with cooked meats, Georgian-style chicken casserole (page 20) or *shashlyk* (page 26) to make a delicious main meal.

What you need

900 g potatoes
pinch of salt
2 onions
4 rashers streaky bacon
4 tbsp milk
1 tbsp plain flour
300 ml soured cream

What you do

1 **Peel** and thinly **slice** the potatoes. Put the potato slices into a saucepan.

2 Cover the potatoes with boiling water. Add a pinch of salt. Bring the water back to the **boil** and cook for 1 minute. **Drain** into a colander.

3 Peel and slice the onions. Cut any rind off the bacon and throw it away. Cut the bacon into small pieces.

4 Next **preheat** the oven to gas mark 5/190 °C/375 °F.

5 Arrange a layer of potato slices in the bottom of a 1.1 litre ovenproof dish. Scatter some onion and bacon on top, and add salt and pepper to taste. Add another layer of potato, then onion and bacon, until they are used up.

6 Pour the milk over the potatoes.

7 In a bowl, stir the flour and soured cream together. Spoon the mixture over all the potatoes, and smooth it with the back of the spoon.

(!) **8** **Cover** the dish with foil and **bake** for 1 hour.

(!) **9** Take the foil off and cook for a further 15 minutes. Serve hot.

Beef Stroganov

There are many tales surrounding the origins of this famous Russian recipe. One tradition is that Count Stroganov, mayor of the city of Odessa during the 1880s, served this dish to anyone tidily dressed who came to his house asking for food. It is a superb main dish, served with rice or potatoes and vegetables.

What you need

2 onions
450 g fillet beef
1 tbsp plain flour
100 g mushrooms
25 g butter
1 beef stock cube
120 ml soured cream
½ tsp cornflour

What you do

1 **Peel** and finely **chop** the onions.

2 Cut the beef into thin slices, and then into thin strips.

3 Put the beef and the flour into a plastic bag. Holding the top closed, shake well to **coat** the beef in the flour.

4 Thinly **slice** the mushrooms.

5 Heat the butter in a frying pan over a medium heat. Add the onions and **fry** for 3–4 minutes, until softened.

6 Using a slotted spoon, lift the onions out of the pan and set aside.

(!) **7** Crumble the stock cube into a measuring jug. Pour in 120 ml **boiling** water and stir until the stock cube is **dissolved**.

(!) **8** Fry the beef in the pan for 3 minutes, stirring from time to time. Add the onions, mushrooms, some salt and pepper, and stock to the pan. **Cover** and **simmer** for 5 minutes.

9 In a small bowl, stir the soured cream and cornflour together. Take the pan off the heat, and stir the soured cream mixture into the beef.

10 Cover and simmer over a low heat for 5 minutes more. Serve hot.

G lushki (Russi n dumplings)

Galushki were traditionally cooked and eaten by poor peasants in Russia. Today, Russian cooks add finely **chopped** meat or vegetables to the basic dumpling mixture as well. Serve them as a snack, or with cooked meat or stews.

What you need

1 onion
125 g butter
 plus 1 tbsp butter
  for **frying**
400 g plain flour
 plus 1 tbsp flour
  for **dusting**
2 tsp caraway seeds
½ tsp salt
2 eggs
142 ml carton
 soured cream

To garnish:
1 tbsp fresh parsley
 or coriander

What you do

1 **Peel** and finely chop the onion.

2 Heat 1 tbsp butter in a pan over a medium heat, and fry the onion for 6–8 minutes, until golden brown. Tip the fried onion into a large bowl.

3 **Sift** the flour into the bowl. Make a dip in the middle.

4 Gradually stir in the caraway seeds, 100 ml water and salt.

5 Cut 100 g of the butter into small pieces and put it into a bowl. **Beat** in the eggs.

6 Add the butter mixture to the flour and mix to a loose dough.

7 Dust a work surface with flour. Roll the dough out until it is ½ cm thick, and then cut it into 2 cm squares.

(!) **8** Bring a large pan of water to the **boil**. Drop the *galushki* into the boiling water and boil for 5 minutes, until they float to the surface. With a slotted spoon, lift them out of the water and into a colander.

(!) **9** Heat the remaining 25 g butter in a frying pan over a medium heat. Add the *galushki* and cook for 2–3 minutes, until they just start to brown.

10 Carefully lift the dumplings into a serving dish. Chop the parsley or coriander.

11 Spoon soured cream on to the dish, sprinkle with chopped parsley or coriander, and serve hot.

Azerbaijan stew

This thick meat stew is a traditional dish in the republic of Azerbaijan, part of the former Soviet Union, to the south-west of Russia. There, the cooking style is influenced by neighbouring countries Iran and Turkey, where fruit is often added to savoury dishes. This recipe makes an ideal main dish, served with bread or rice.

What you need

250 g neck fillet lamb
  or cold, cooked lamb
1 onion
4 chestnuts (if available)
4 dried apricots
2 tbsp butter
1 lamb or vegetable
  stock cube
1 tbsp fresh parsley
1 tbsp fresh coriander
1 tbsp tomato purée
½ tbsp fresh thyme
50 g lentils
8 new potatoes

*To **garnish**:*
sprigs of fresh parsley
  and coriander

What you do

1 Cut any fat from the lamb and throw it away. Cut the meat into 1 cm cubes.

2 **Peel** and **chop** the onion.

3 Peel and chop the chestnuts roughly (if you are using them). Chop the dried apricots.

(!) 4 Heat the butter in a saucepan over a medium heat. **Fry** the onion for 3 minutes.

5 Add the lamb and cook until each cube is turning brown.

6 Crumble the stock cube into a measuring jug with 600 ml hot water and stir well. Chop the parsley and coriander.

(!) **7** Add the stock cube, apricots, chestnuts, tomato purée, parsley, coriander, thyme, lentils and potatoes to the meat. Stir well and bring to the **boil**. **Cover** and **simmer** for 20 minutes.

8 Take the pan off the heat. Cut the potatoes in the pan into bite-sized pieces.

9 Spoon the stew into bowls, and garnish with sprigs of fresh parsley and coriander.

Curd cheese tarts

In Russia, these tarts are often served with tea, called *chai* (pronounced *cha-ee*). Tea drinking is an important occasion in Russia, and can last a long time. In summer, people drink their *chai* ice-cold, as a refreshing drink.

What you need

200 g plain flour
 plus 1 tbps flour
   for **dusting**
½ tsp baking powder
50 g butter
1 large egg
100 ml soured cream
200 g curd cheese
   or quark
1 tsp caster sugar

What you do

1 **Sift** the flour and baking powder into a bowl.

2 Cut the butter into cubes and add it to the flour. Rub it between your fingertips until the mixture looks like breadcrumbs.

3 **Beat** the egg lightly in a cup. Stir a third of the egg and all of the soured cream into the flour mixture.

4 Shape the mixture into a ball. **Cover** it with clingfilm and **chill** for 30 minutes.

5 Meanwhile, put the curd cheese into a sieve and let it **drain** for 5 minutes. Tip the cheese, another third of the egg and the caster sugar into a bowl and mix well. Chill for 15 minutes.

6 **Preheat** the oven to gas mark 6/200 °C/400 °F.

7 Dust a work surface with a little flour. Roll the pastry out until it is 3 mm thick. Using pastry cutters, cut out eight 9 cm rounds and eight 6 cm rounds.

8 Put 1½ tbsp curd cheese mixture into the middle of each larger round.

9 Brush the edges of each larger circle with some beaten egg. Put a smaller round on top. Join the edges by pinching them together.

10 Put the tarts on to a baking tray and brush them with the remaining beaten egg.

11 **Bake** for 15–20 minutes, until golden. Serve warm or cold, with fresh fruit.

Paska (Curd cheese cake)

Paska, (pronounced *PA-ska*) is usually made inside a carved wooden mould, and decorated with nuts and glacé fruits. It is traditionally eaten at Easter. Glacé fruit are dipped into a sugary syrup, dried and then dipped again. This recipe uses an empty cream or yoghurt pot as the mould.

What you need

400 g curd cheese or quark
4 eggs
4 tbsp soured cream
50 g raisins
3 tbsp caster sugar
50 g blanched almonds
1 tbsp candied orange peel
  or grated lemon rind

To decorate:
glacé cherries, blanched
  almonds, angelica,
  candied orange and
  lemon peel

What you do

1 Put the curd cheese in a sieve and leave it to **drain** for 3 hours.

2 Lightly **beat** the eggs. Put them into a bowl with the soured cream and curd cheese.

(!) 3 Set the bowl over a pan which has a little hot water in the bottom. Allowing the water to **simmer** over a medium heat, stir the curd cheese mixture for about 15 minutes, until it starts to thicken.

(!) 4 Take the pan off the heat. Wearing oven gloves, lift the bowl off. Stir the raisins and sugar into the cheese.

5 Roughly **chop** the almonds – you can also do this in a blender. Stir them and the candied orange peel into the curd cheese, and leave to cool.

6 Make a few small holes in the bottom of a 568 ml cream or yoghurt pot. Line it with a piece of muslin or a clean tea towel.

7 Spoon the cheese mixture into the pot, smoothing the surface. Put a small plate on top and a can of food on top of the plate, to press the mixture. **Chill** overnight.

8 Turn the paska on to a serving plate. Lift off the cloth, and decorate the sides with patterns of almonds and glacé fruits.

St Petersburg-style apples

Apples are plentiful in the autumn in many parts of Russia, and baked apples are a popular dessert. This version of **baking** them comes from the city of St Petersburg in north-west Russia. Here, the apples are filled with vanilla-flavoured sugar and wrapped in strips of puff pastry.

What you need

4 eating apples
4 tsp caster sugar
1 tsp vanilla extract
1 tbsp flour for **dusting**
300 g ready-made
   puff pastry
1 egg

To decorate:
sprigs of fresh mint

What you do

1 Using an apple corer, push down through each apple until the corer is about 2 cm above the bottom of the fruit. Lift out the top part of the core, leaving the last section still inside.

2 Put 1 tsp caster sugar into the hollow in each apple. Drip a few drops of vanilla extract on to the sugar.

3 Dust a work surface with the flour. Roll the pastry out until it is 3 mm thick. Cut it into 2 cm wide strips.

4 Crack the egg into a cup and **beat** it with a fork.

40

5 Brush one strip of pastry with egg. Wind it around the bottom of the apple, with the eggy side next to the apple. Do the same with another strip of pastry, overlapping it with the first one slightly. Do this until the apple is covered.

6 Repeat step 5 for the other apples.

7 Brush the pastry with beaten egg and put the apples onto a baking tray. **Chill** for 30 minutes.

8 **Preheat** the oven to gas mark 7/210 °C/425 °F. Bake the apples for 20–25 minutes, until golden. Allow to cool slightly before decorating with mint and serving with cream.

Cherry kissel

Kissel gets its name from the Russian word for sour, *kisly* (pronounced *KEES-lee*). This version uses cherries, but you can make kissel from plums, damsons or any berry fruits. It is a little like a runny fruit jelly. Russian cooks use flour made from potatoes to thicken the fruit juice, but you can use cornflour if you cannot find potato flour.

What you need

450 g morello cherries
100 g caster sugar
1½ tbsp potato flour
   or cornflour
1 tsp vanilla extract

What you do

1 Rinse the cherries. Using a small, sharp knife, cut the cherries in half and lift out the stones. Put the cherries into a bowl.

2 Put 600 ml water into a saucepan. Stir in the sugar and add the cherries. **Cover** and **simmer** over a low heat for 10 minutes.

3 In a cup, mix the potato flour or cornflour and 2 tbsp cold water into a paste. Stir this into the cherries.

(!) **4** Bring to the **boil** and simmer for 2 minutes. Stir in the vanilla extract.

5 Pour the kissel into a serving dish and leave to cool for at least 1 hour, before **chilling** for 30 minutes. Serve with cream.

WOODLAND FOODS

Russian cooks traditionally find many cooking ingredients growing wild, in woods. These include all sorts of berries, hazelnuts and mushrooms.

Further information

Here are some places to find out more about Russia and Russian cooking.

Books

DK Eyewitness Guides: Russia, Kathleen Berton Murrell (Dorling Kindersley, 1998)
Next Stop! Russia, Fred Martin (Heinemann Library, 1997)
Russian Cookbook, Kyra Petrovskaya (Dover Publications, 1992)

Websites

www.britannia.org/recipes/russian
www.russianembassy.org/RUSSIA/cuisine.htm
www.russia-in-us.com

Conversion chart

Ingredients for recipes can be measured in two different ways. Metric measurements use grams and millilitres. Imperial measurements use ounces and fluid ounces. This book uses metric measurements. The chart here shows you how to convert measurements from metric to imperial.

SOLIDS		LIQUIDS	
METRIC	IMPERIAL	METRIC	IMPERIAL
10 g	¼ oz	30 ml	1 fl oz
15 g	½ oz	50 ml	2 fl oz
25 g	1 oz	75 ml	2½ fl oz
50 g	1¾ oz	100 ml	3½ fl oz
75 g	2¾ oz	125 ml	4 fl oz
100 g	3½ oz	150 ml	5 fl oz
150 g	5 oz	300 ml	10 fl oz
250 g	9 oz	600 ml	20 fl oz
450 g	16 oz		

Healthy eating

This diagram shows which foods you should eat to stay healthy. Most of your food should come from the bottom of the pyramid. Eat some of the foods from the middle every day. Only eat a little of the foods from the top.

Healthy eating, Russian-style

Russian meals include a lot of bread, made with flour from wheat, oat or rye grains, from the bottom layer of the pyramid. People eat whatever fresh fruit and vegetables are available, storing ones that will keep to eat during the winter, when there is less choice. Russian cookery uses different kinds of soft cheeses and thick, soured cream, which should only be eaten from time to time.

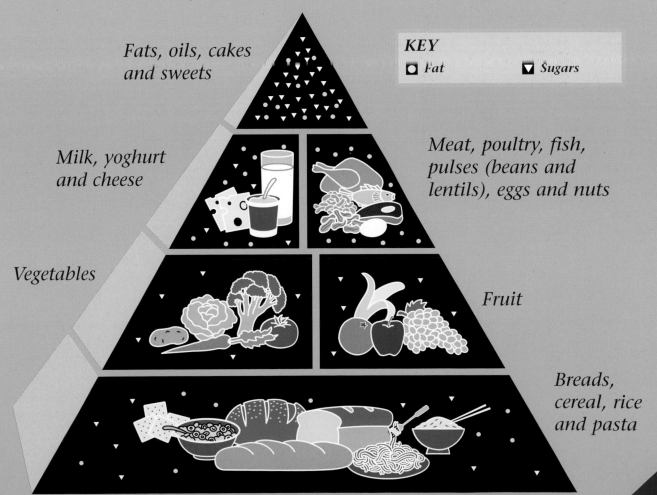

Fats, oils, cakes and sweets

KEY
☐ Fat   ▼ Sugars

Milk, yoghurt and cheese

Meat, poultry, fish, pulses (beans and lentils), eggs and nuts

Vegetables

Fruit

Breads, cereal, rice and pasta

Glossary

bacteria tiny organisms that can be added to food to alter its taste, for example, turning cream sour.

bake cook something in the oven

barbecue cooked outside on a grid fixed over burning charcoal

beat mix ingredients together strongly, using a fork or whisk

blend mix ingredients together in a blender or food processor

boil cook a liquid on the hob. Boiling liquid bubbles and steams strongly.

chill put a dish in the fridge for a while before serving

chop cut into pieces using a sharp knife

coat cover with a mixture or sauce

communists people who believe the government should own all businesses and property, and provide work for the people

cover put a lid on a pan, or put foil or clingfilm over a dish

deciduous trees which lose their leaves each autumn are deciduous

dissolve mix something, such as sugar, so that it disappears into a liquid

drain remove liquid, usually by pouring something into a colander or sieve

dust sprinkle flour or icing sugar over something

fertile good for growing things in

fry cook something in oil in a pan

garnish decorate food, for example, with fresh herbs

grate break something, such as cheese, into small pieces using a grater

grill cook under a grill

ground crushed into small pieces or powder

knead press and fold with the hands

marinade sauce that meat is soaked in before cooking, to make it tender

peel remove the skin of a fruit or vegetable

preheat turn on the oven in advance, so that is it hot when you are ready to use it

roasted cooked in a very hot oven

shred cut something into thin strips

sift remove lumps from dry ingredients, such as flour, with a sieve

simmer cook liquid on the hob. Simmering liquid bubbles and steams gently.

slice cut into thin flat pieces

Index